Number in the Nursery and Reception

a framework for supporting and assessing number learning

Sue Gifford with Patti Barber and Sheila Ebbutt

BEAM

Published by BEAM Education, Maze Workshops, 72a Southgate Road, London N1 3JT
Copyright © BEAM 1998
Cover illustration © Beverly Levy, 12 Shipton Street, London E2 7RU
Photographs on pp 50, 51 and 59 © Catherine Clark; other photographs © Sally Greenhill
All rights reserved

British Library Cataloguing-in Publication Data
A catalogue record for this book is available from the British Library.

ISBN 978 1 8740 9969 7

Designed and typeset by BEAM and Bookcraft, Stroud
Printed by Five Castles Press, Duke Street, Ipswich, IP3 0AG
Reprinted in 2007

Contents

Introduction

New thinking about children's number learning

This book is intended for adults working with three- to five-year-olds, who wish to know how to provide help with learning about number. It is based on current thinking, which differs from previous approaches to young children's number learning in two important ways:

- firstly, it is now agreed that we should not limit our expectations of young children on the basis of their age alone. Children learn about numeracy from an early age, and do not need to be restricted to learning about matching and sets first, or working only with small numbers. We need to find out about, and develop, each individual child's understanding of number

- secondly, young children learn about the importance of the number system from their social experience, and from people who demonstrate its usefulness and interest value

It follows from this that we need to:

- find out as much as we can about the individual child's experiences and understanding of number, both from parents and carers and from our own observations

- find ways of showing children the various purposes and meanings of numbers, and their fascinating patterns and properties

Number and mathematics

There is more to mathematics than just number, but number is nonetheless a very important aspect of mathematics. Developing number understanding gives opportunities to develop wider aspects of mathematics, such as logical reasoning, pattern spotting, abstract thinking and problem solving. It also helps develop communication skills through language and symbols.

In current thinking, confidence in number is an important aim in the curriculum for three- to five-year-olds. The new approach to numeracy in the early years acknowledges that traditional expectations of children's abilities may have been set too low. By drawing on children's experiences and interest in big numbers, and by making use of language, practical activities and problem solving, we can help them to fulfill their potential.

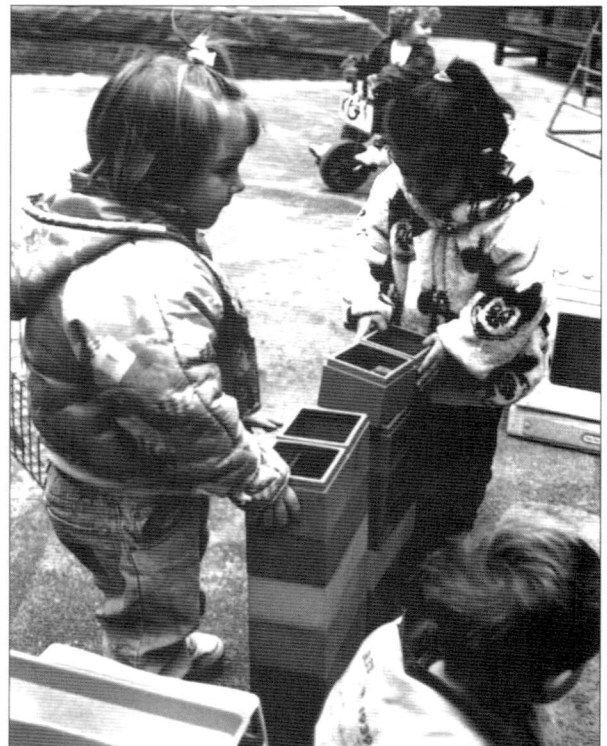

How many bricks are there in your tower?

A non-hierarchical list

Children's learning about number is not strictly hierarchical. The various aspects of number are generally learned simultaneously.

Our aim as teachers should be to create a stimulating, number-rich environment, in which children become familiar with written numerals and have real purposes for counting and calculating. This helps each child to learn the different aspects of number at his or her own pace. While still getting to know the small numbers they may learn to add or subtract one or two, recite numbers over 20, and become familiar with written number symbols.

A good start to number

One of the aims of mathematics education in early childhood is for children to see maths as interesting, relevant, enjoyable and worthwhile: finding that numbers can amuse, delight, illuminate and explain.

Te Whariki – The New Zealand Early Childhood Guidelines

All children are entitled to learn about mathematics, including number. As with literacy, children who come from homes where numbers are part of everyday life and conversation have the advantage of a positive attitude to numeracy from the start.

If we want all children to start off in this way, we need to provide experiences which develop their positive attitudes and understanding. Some children avoid activities involving numbers, making comments such as "I'm not very good at counting" or "I can't do numbers". It is obviously important that children are not pressurised into learning about numbers, or taught in ways which do not relate to their experience and understanding. But we must be careful not to collude with their low self-esteem by offering only simplified and unchallenging activities.

Sammy, at 5, has obviously learnt about numbers at home. He shows particular interest in large numbers, incorporating them into his pictures at every opportunity.

About this book

This book is divided into three main sections covering the broad areas of mathematical experience that children encounter at nursery level. These are: Counting; Representing Numbers; and Number Patterns and Problems.

Each section is introduced by a Contents page which lists the topics covered, and the learning objectives for each topic.

A short introduction to the section then follows, which explains the mathematics covered and outlines important points to bear in mind when teaching.

Four pages of activities are then given for each topic. The first two pages, 'Opportunities', suggest ways of working with the relevant mathematics through various nursery activities. Finally, one activity is presented in more detail on the last two pages of each topic.

A key to the page layout of the book is given below.

The 'Opportunities' pages

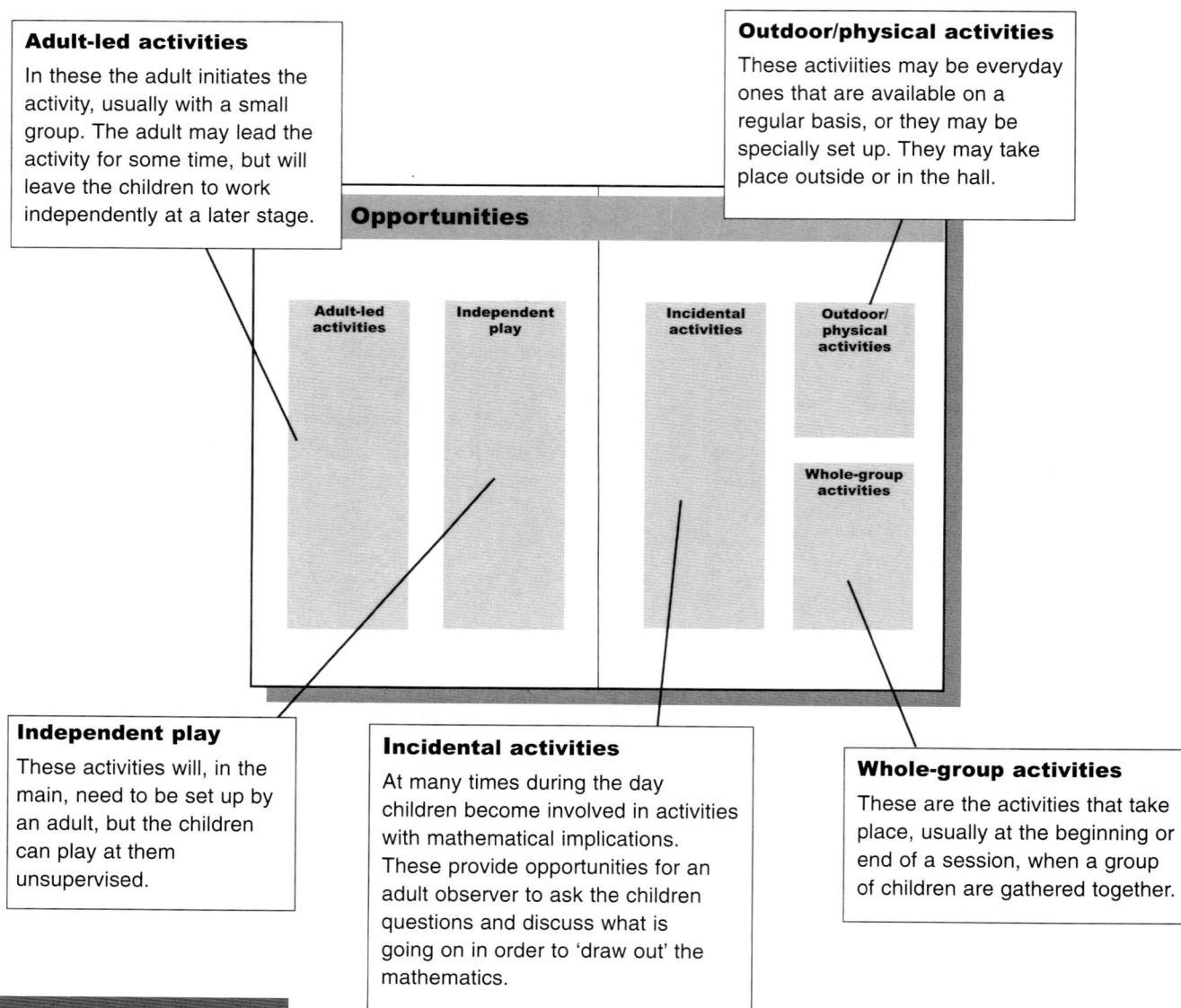

Adult-led activities

In these the adult initiates the activity, usually with a small group. The adult may lead the activity for some time, but will leave the children to work independently at a later stage.

Outdoor/physical activities

These activiities may be everyday ones that are available on a regular basis, or they may be specially set up. They may take place outside or in the hall.

Opportunities

Adult-led activities

Independent play

Incidental activities

Outdoor/ physical activities

Whole-group activities

Independent play

These activities will, in the main, need to be set up by an adult, but the children can play at them unsupervised.

Incidental activities

At many times during the day children become involved in activities with mathematical implications. These provide opportunities for an adult observer to ask the children questions and discuss what is going on in order to 'draw out' the mathematics.

Whole-group activities

These are the activities that take place, usually at the beginning or end of a session, when a group of children are gathered together.

The 'Activity' and 'What to look for' pages

These pages provide detailed help with one activity, providing support with the introduction and development of the mathematics involved, and pointers for observation and assessment.

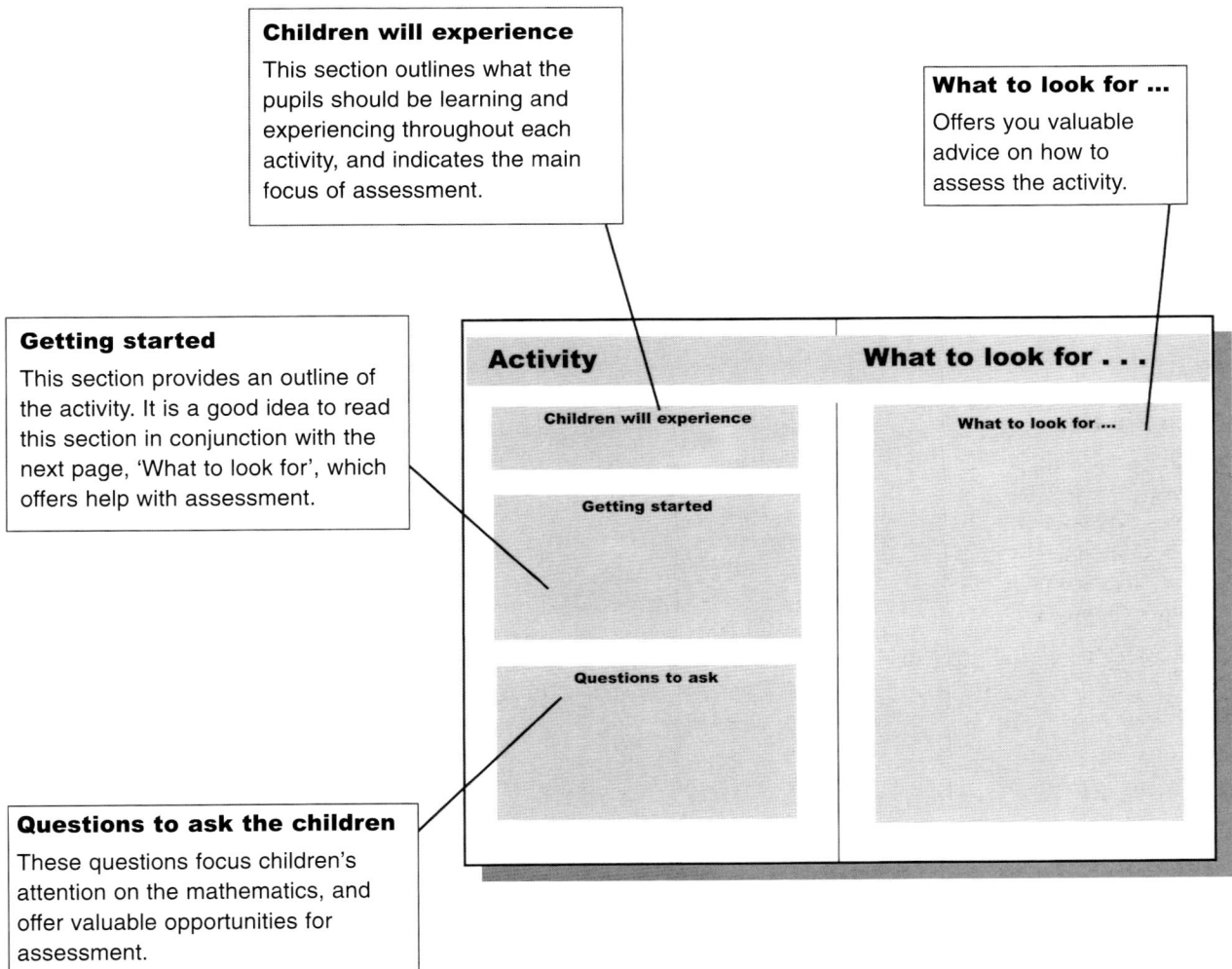

Children will experience
This section outlines what the pupils should be learning and experiencing throughout each activity, and indicates the main focus of assessment.

What to look for ...
Offers you valuable advice on how to assess the activity.

Getting started
This section provides an outline of the activity. It is a good idea to read this section in conjunction with the next page, 'What to look for', which offers help with assessment.

Activity

Children will experience

Getting started

Questions to ask

What to look for . . .

What to look for ...

Questions to ask the children
These questions focus children's attention on the mathematics, and offer valuable opportunities for assessment.

'Checklist' pages

You will find on pages 62 and 63 a checklist, which is intended to define teaching objectives within each mathematical area. It is hoped that this list will provide a comprehensive reference for teachers, which can be used as a basis for planning and assessment, as well as representing a clear focus for each set of activities.

Counting

Counting

Important aspects of counting

The Number Sequence
◆ *knowing some numbers*

◆ *knowing the order of the number names*

◆ *knowing what number comes next*

◆ *knowing ordinal numbers (first, second, and so on)*

◆ *knowing the decades*

Organising Counting
◆ *synchronising number words and pointing*

◆ *counting each item once and once only*

Understanding Counting
◆ *saying how many there are*

◆ *counting a number of things*

Purposes for Counting
◆ *understanding why we need to count*

Counting and cardinal number

In order to count, children need to be able to:

• say the numbers in sequence

• organise their counting (that is, say one number for each object, and keep track of which things they've counted)

• understand that the last number they say gives the number in the set

The last point describes the idea of cardinal number. If you ask children who have just counted some objects, "So how many are there?" those who understand cardinality are more likely to say the number — others will start counting again or just say any number. A good way to find out whether children really understand cardinality is to ask them to get you six plates from a large pile. Some will just 'grab' an approximate number while others will count; children are sometimes described as 'grabbers' or 'counters' according to their response to this sort of request.

Children show an understanding of counting when they are able to tell you how many of something there are. They are using counting for their own purposes: to get the 'right number', or to check it. Once they reach this stage, they are also likely to understand that, if things are rearranged, counting them again will give the same number. This is the idea of the invariance, or conservation, of number.

The sequence of numbers

Children often go through a stage where they know some numbers which they say in random order, such as "1, 2, 3, 7, 5, 8". Before they progress from here, children need to learn how to say the number names in sequence, and to synchronise their counting and pointing, keeping track of what they have counted. These are difficult things to learn and should not be underestimated as achievements for children, and for the parents who have helped them to learn these skills.

Just saying which number comes next in a sequence can be hard. For instance, if you ask children "what comes after 6?", some will count from one and say "1, 2, 3, 4, 5, 6, 7". This is sometimes called counting in a 'string'. If children can just say the next number, '7', they are using numbers as a 'chain', which is a significant achievement.

At a later stage children counting up to 20 must recognise the strange pattern of the teen numbers: 12, 13, 14, 15, which should logically be 'twoteen, threeteen, fourteen, fiveteen' in order to be consistent with the higher teen numbers.

The meaning of the 'teen' as ten is not obvious either, and will probably only be appreciated much later.

Another pattern has to be learned on reaching the numbers in the twenties. In order to generate the pattern which enables children to say numbers to 100, they have to learn the pattern 'umpty-one, umpty-two, umpty-three …', and dovetail it with the pattern of the tens numbers, 'twenty, thirty, forty …'. (This pattern of tens numbers is not regular either. Arguably the numbers should be 'twoty, threety, fourty, fivety, sixty …'. The difficulty of fitting the two patterns together is indicated by children's tendency to get stuck at 29 or 39, when they need to produce the relevant 'tens' number and insert it into the pattern: 27, 28, 29. A child's logical solution to this problem is often to count 'twenty-seven, twenty-eight, twenty-nine, twenty-ten'.

Purposes for counting

Children need to learn that counting is useful — for themselves and for adults — in order to appreciate its function and to be interested in learning about it. Adults need to be positive role models and make it explicit when they are counting for a purpose, as well as providing opportunities for children to count purposefully.

Generally, people need to count when a number of things is too big to judge by eye. For most people this will be numbers over three, unless things are arranged in a pattern. There is some evidence that young children can assess a larger number of objects without counting if they are able to group them: for instance, recognising 6 as 3 and 3.

There are two main purposes for counting: firstly, when an exact number is required (for example, only six people can make dough at once); and secondly, when checking to see whether there are the same number of things ("I've got four sweets but you've got five, so it's not fair").

Young children rarely count things: more often they use number to assert status ("I'm four and you're only three"). As teachers we should provide opportunities for children to see the need to count, so that they come to appreciate what counting is for. This means involving children in preparing, organising and tidying up after activities where numbers are involved, as well as actually playing the games.

Ordinal number

It is important that children have experience of hearing and then using ordinal numbers such as 'first', 'second' 'third'. Ordinal numbers can be used incidentally when children come into the room in the morning. "Who was first today? Who was second? … Who will be fifth?" Planning the day provides another opportunity. "What shall we do first? … And second? And then? … What shall we do last?"

Children often enjoy counting just to demonstrate and practise their skills. This child counted the trays and wrote the total number, 19.

The number sequence

Independent play

Sand-timers

Put out a range of sand-timers and encourage the children to see how far they can count before the sand runs out.

Hide and seek

Encourage children to play games like 'Hide and Seek'. This will give them an opportunity to practise saying numbers in sequence. If they are not sure of the numbers to twenty, they might count to ten twice, or they could count in pairs to support each other.

Water tray

Provide materials for children to act out the story of 'Five Speckled Frogs' on a log (or lily pad). This gives experience of counting forwards and backwards.

Incidental activity

By the time I've counted to ...

Ask children to come and sit down, put their games away or finish their pictures "By the time I've counted to 5 (or 10, 20, 30)."

Making models

Discuss the order of doing things. What needs to be done first, and why? What will you do second? And third?

Changing for PE

Talk about the order of taking garments off, or putting them on. "What do you take off first? Does it matter? What do you take off next?"

This child talked about the ages of members of her family, saying that Mummy was 29 and Yolande was six. She was able to say who was older than herself, and who was younger.

Outdoor/physical activity

Various games

Various activities lend themselves to counting:

- giant-striding, pigeon-stepping
- bouncing balls, throwing and catching
- using a 'hitting line' where children hit objects tied to a clothes line, using a bat
- jumping into hoops laid in a trail, or from skittle to skittle in a line

Children could be helped to record their highest numbers, (see suggestions for scoring in the 'Representing Numbers' section).

Television

Programmes such as BBC's 'Number Time', or 'Sesame Street', offer rhymes and tunes for children to count to.

Reciting number rhymes.

Whole group activity

Rhymes

Many rhymes and stories practise the sequence of numbers forwards and backwards. Examples are: 'Once I Caught a Fish Alive', 'Five Speckled Frogs'; 'Five Little Ducks'; 'This Old Man'; and 'Ten Green Bottles'. You might record rhymes on tape for children to play or take home.

You can increase the numbers in rhymes or just practise counting from different starting points — forwards and backwards from 10 or 20, for example.

Spot the mistake; Missing number

Say the numbers in order, but include a deliberate mistake. Children enjoy identifying where you have missed numbers out or got them in the wrong order, and this is useful for getting them to focus on the sequence.

Clapping rhythms

It is easier for children to remember a sequence such as the counting numbers if they associate it with a regular rhythm. You can help children count and clap: "1 (pause) 2 (pause) 3, 4, 5 (pause) 6 (pause) 7 (pause) 8, 9, 10" or have a regular beat which emphasises the verbal pattern of the teens and twenties.

You can also use tambourines or drums to keep rhythms going.

The number sequence
Activity: Hop, skip and jump

Children will experience

◆ saying the numbers in sequence
(but not necessarily synchronising
numbers with actions)

Equipment

◆ skipping ropes

◆ tracks on the ground (chalked or
painted with powder paint)

Getting started

In the playground, children count how many times they can hop, jump or skip without
stopping. This is a good opportunity for group counting, where the teacher and other
children watch and count along while one child skips in a big rope, or children take
turns to hop along a trail of 'stepping stones'.

This activity is about saying the number sequence and not about counting objects, so
don't worry if children's recitation of the number names does not correspond entirely
with their actions: accurate counting comes later.

Some schools have permanent playground markings, such as tracks on the ground,
which could be used for this activity. Alternatively you could make some with chalk or
paint, or children could use paving stones. Children who recognise symbols can use
these to support their counting of higher numbers.

Questions to ask the children

What number comes next?

Can you carry on counting without going back to one?

How many jumps did you do?
How many do you think you will do next time?

Can you say the numbers as you jump from slab to slab?

What number can you count up to while you skip round the playground?

Can you hop along this track all the way to the end, and say the numbers as you go?

Can you jump from skittle to skittle, and count as you go?

Where did your first jump land? Your second, third ...?

What to look for . . .

About the number sequence	the children may . . .	if so . . .	In counting generally
	show no interest	try to find a context for counting which will appeal more — or try again another day	
knowing some numbers	say some number names, but miss some out or say them in the wrong order	give them more experience of singing, chanting and saying the number names, with actions and body movements	
	consistently count with a sequence of their own, such as '1, 2, 3, 7, 8'	talk to them about these numbers; it may be that they are using numbers that have a personal significance for them, such as door numbers	
	use the number names in order, but either use too many numbers for the objects, or miss some objects out	choose some activities from the section 'Organising Counting'	organising counting
	seem unable to say how many they have just counted	choose some activities from the section 'Understanding Counting'	understanding counting
knowing the order of the number names	count confidently and with sequences of numbers higher than you would expect	develop flexibility in counting by asking them to count forwards from a number without going back to one, or to count backwards	
		help them to go on to spot the verbal patterns in the teens and twenties numbers	purposes for counting
knowing what comes next	show their awareness of patterns, by inventing their own, for instance by counting 'fourteen, fiveteen' or 'twenty-nine, twenty-ten'	start counting at ten or twenty, and rehearse the pattern of 'twenty, thirty, forty', then combine this with the pairs 'twenty-nine, thirty, thirty-nine, forty'	

You can help the children to count objects by encouraging them to arrange items in a row, point as they count, move the objects in time with counting, and make exaggerated rhythmic actions as they count.

Adult-led activities

Playing games

Games where children throw dice and count a number of moves along a track will help them to coordinate their counting with pointing movements. Asking them to predict where they will land helps them focus on the purpose of the game.

You can make your own large-scale table-top games to suit current interests and resources by simply drawing a track with a felt-tipped pen on kitchen paper covering a table.

Games where children collect counters (or other items) to match the spaces on a base board provide particularly useful practice in counting objects (see for instance *Early Birds* from Adam Toys or *Bright Ideas* maths games).

Houses for bears

Children make 'houses' with Clixi and then count how many little plastic bears will fit in. This is an activity which combines spatial creativity (in making the different-shaped houses) with counting.

Boxes can also be made with other apparatus and then filled with other animal counters or other small objects.

In the jar

Fill a jar with conkers, soft toys, apples … (you can use big or small things, depending on whether you want a lower or higher number of objects). Ask the children to guess how many things are in the jar, and then count to check.

Independent play

Abacus and beads

The traditional abacus provides a model of counting by moving things in a row one at a time.

Beads on strings provide the same opportunities; children can make patterns on necklaces and count the numbers of colours and shapes used.

Other opportunities

Computer programmes like 'Animated Number' provide irregular arrangements of things to count.

Sand tray

Put three goats, a bridge and a troll in the sand tray and children can act out the story of 'The Three Billy Goats Gruff'.

Mina drew some shapes, then counted them vigorously, pointing to each one in turn.

Outdoor/physical activities

Hoops, tracks, skipping ...

Counting while jumping in hoops or along tracks outside helps children to coordinate moves and counting.

Giant board games

You could create large versions of board games, where the children themselves are the 'counters'.

Large shapes

Put large shapes on the floor and let children throw a large dice to determine how many shapes to jump on.

Some children become very involved in drawing sets of nesting shapes, and enjoy counting how many they can fit inside the original shape. Edward made certain he had counted every shape by marking each one with a blob.

Whole-group activities

Stories and number books

Children enjoy simple counting books, especially of the pop-up variety, at story-time.

These offer counting pictures which are arranged haphazardly, giving the opportunity to demonstrate how to be systematic and keep track of which things have been counted and which have not.

Counting children

Ask one child to count everyone in the group by touching them on the head. When children have been counted, they stand up. This encourages the children to participate, and to coordinate their counting with the touching, which makes the 'one-number, one-object' message very clear.

Listening to counting stories.

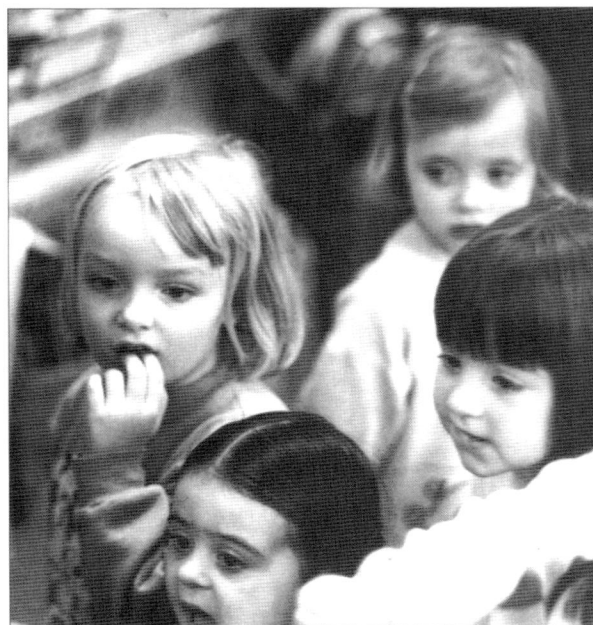

Organising counting
Activity: Baskets

Children will experience

◆ ways of organising counting

◆ counting with no purpose: just for fun

Equipment

◆ containers such as boxes and baskets

◆ collections of things such as buttons and shells

Getting started

Provide baskets containing different collections of things (buttons, shells, pine cones, assorted small teddy bears, tiny tins of food …), and natural groups relating to current interests, like dolls in a family, seeds in a piece of fruit, peas in a pod, seeds in a sunflower head, and so on. Encourage the children to estimate, and then count, how many objects there are in the basket or group of objects they have chosen.

Questions to ask the children

Can you move them as you count?

Did you count this one?
How do you know?

Did you miss any out?
How do you know?

How could we make sure we've counted them all and not missed any out?

Would it help to put them in a line?
In a group?
In pairs?

Can we still count them if they are arranged in a circle?
Or higgledy-piggledy?

What to look for . . .

Organising counting	the children may . . .	if so . . .	In counting generally
	sort the objects instead of counting	leave them to do it, and observe counting another time	
	say one number for one object, but not know all the number names	choose some activities from the 'Number Sequence' section	number sequence
synchronising the saying of numbers with pointing	miss some objects out, count some twice, or carry on counting after they've finished counting them all	suggest that they arrange objects in a line to make them easier to count	
	count inaccurately without touching or moving the objects	suggest that they touch them with exaggerated movements in a steady rhythm	
counting each item once and once only	count accurately	offer further challenges, such as counting objects arranged in a circle, or pictures in which objects are placed higgledy-piggledy	
	emphasise or repeat the last number when they've counted	the children may know that the last number they say tells them the number in the group (the idea of cardinal number); they may just say the last number because adults do this, so you could ask, "So how many are there?" If they cannot tell how many there are after counting, choose some activities from the 'Understanding Counting' section	understanding counting

Many of the activities already suggested in this section provide opportunities for counting. The important thing is to encourage children to draw conclusions about how many items there are altogether: if they have counted every object in a group, saying "One, two, three", then there are three things altogether. You can help them reach this conclusion by saying, for instance, "You counted up to five. So there are five cars altogether", or "You counted to three. So how many people are there? ... Yes, three." This can help clarify for the children the point that the last number name they said is the number of things in the group.

Asking children to fetch you a number of objects — say, four cups, or six hats, encourages them to focus on getting the right number of objects, rather than on the counting process alone.

Adult-led activities

Shop

Model the process of shopping for the children by sitting down in the class shop and counting out pennies as they are given to the 'shopkeeper'.

Party in the home corner

Set out a certain number of dolls for children to lay the table for.

Noises

Drop noisy objects into a bucket. Ask "How many did I put in?". Try the same thing with quieter objects.

Water tray

Ask children "How many jugs of water does it take to fill up the water tray?", and help them to find out the answer.

Washing line game

Roll a large foam dice, collect the number of dirty clothes indicated on the dice, and hang them on the line.

Independent play

Matching cards

You need sets of cards, each showing a different picture for the same number (three ladybirds, three cats, three books; four ladders, four dogs, four people ...).

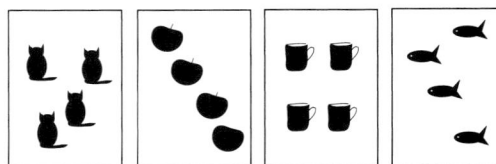

To start with, only use cards with three or four things on for children to sort. These can be displayed for matching and sorting. Later children can sort collections of threes, fours and fives, or twos, fours and eights.

This child drew a box, then decorated her picture. She counted the different kinds of pattern she had used, and announced "There are eight patterns on the lid".

Opportunities for counting to see how many objects there are, and for counting a given number from larger group

Incidental activities

Washing Lego (or other equipment)

Ask children "How many pieces have we washed?". In this situation, children may naturally comment on the large amount of pieces.

Baskets

Give children baskets and bags to fill with things in the role play area. Ask "How many things have you got in your basket? Have you got more than, or fewer than, your friend?"

Water tray

Children can count how many jugs of water it takes to fill the water tray.

Building

When children build a big tower with bricks, they are often interested in the large numbers involved. "Can you count how many bricks you have used?"

The natural world

Talk with the children about:

- how many chicks have hatched
- how many seeds have germinated
- how many tomatoes there are on the plant
- how many babies the guinea pig had
- how many frogs have developed

Small world

When children play with toy farms, houses, shops or garages, ask: "How many pigs are there in the pigsty?" "How many cars are on the road?" "How many people are in that bus?"

Outdoor/physical activities

How many have I found/dug up?

Children digging or looking for minibeasts outdoors will find plenty of opportunities for discussing how many worms or ladybirds they have found, and which there are most of.

Beanbags in the bucket

Children count how many beanbags they can throw in a bucket. This gives a purpose for counting in an activity using large motor skills. Similar activities include: throwing hoops over cones; balls into a basket-ball net; scoring goals.

Trikes

"How many trikes are there? So how many children can have a trike?" "How many turns have you had on the trikes this morning?"

Whole-group activity

Rhymes

'Five Currant Buns' and similar rhymes and stories offer plenty of opportunities for asking "How many are there now?". Children can hold large currant buns made from card or fabric, and discuss how many there are each time.

Understanding counting

Children will experience

◆ counting objects

◆ counting out a number of objects

◆ saying how many there are

◆ comparing numbers

Equipment

◆ jackets cut out of card, each with ten button holes

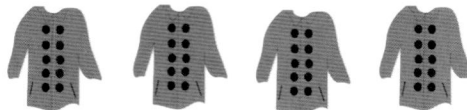

◆ assorted buttons

◆ ordinary dice with spots

◆ a shaker (any pot will do)

Getting started

Each child has a jacket cut out of card. They take it in turns to toss the dice, say the number, and take that number of buttons. (Children enjoy using a shaker and turning it over on the table to trap and then reveal the dice — which also keeps it under control.) The aim is to collect enough buttons to complete the jacket.

Children can choose another jacket when they have finished.

Questions to ask the children

What number is on the dice?

How many buttons should you get?

How many more buttons do you need to fill all your button holes?

Which jacket has more buttons?

Understanding counting		the children may . . .	if so . . .	In counting generally
		just fill the jackets' button holes without counting	talk about what they have done, leave them to it, and see if they will focus on counting another time	
saying how many there are		count with a non-standard sequence of numbers	choose some activities from the section 'Number Sequence'	number sequence
		not coordinate saying the numbers with touching the spots or buttons	choose some activities from the section 'Organising Counting'	organising counting
		count the spots on the dice, but not know how many buttons they need	encourage children to focus on the required number and realise that the last number they say tells them the number on the dice face, and the number of buttons they need	
counting out a number of things		count past the number required	the children may need to develop more confidence in just saying the numbers. Point out that the last number they say is the number in the group (the cardinal idea of number): '1, 2, 3' means there are 3 altogether. Try again with a dice showing a smaller number of dots, such as just 1, 2 and 3	purposes for counting
		self-correct, check by recounting or correct other children's responses	children who do this usually understand that counting is a useful technique for finding out how many there are. Check with some activities from the section 'Purposes for Counting'	
		just grab a number of buttons	show children that counting will get them the right number of buttons	

You can help children to learn why we count by modelling the process for them. Show them by example that counting is useful for various purposes: to find out how many things there are in a group (counting the conkers collected in the park); to collect the right number of the things we need (counting out three cupfuls of flour, getting six aprons for six children); and to check that we have not lost anything (counting the teddies at tidying-up time).

Adult-led activities

Cooking

Cooking offers real opportunities to count. Children need to check that the right number of cupfuls, spoonfuls or eggs are used for the recipe.

Birthday cake

Put the right number of candles on the cake.

Five children only

An activity like cooking or making playdough is only feasible with limited numbers of children at a time. This provides a good opportunity for children to see the purpose of counting, and to check whether more children can join the group or if there are enough already.

Teddy bears' picnic

How many plates do we need so that the bears have one each?

How many biscuits do we need so that they can have three each?

We have 12 raisins. We must share them fairly between the bears, then check by counting the raisins on each plate.

Independent play

Making models and constructions

Children who are planning these can say in advance how many pieces they need — for instance, how many wheels they will need to make a car.

Imaginative play areas

Shops, cafes, or fast food counters will engage the children in asking for numbers of things. For instance, if they are in a family group, they can decide how many drinks or sandwiches they need, and check whether or not the shop assistant has given them the right number. They can also play with the right number of pennies or plastic pounds.

Symmetrical patterns

Making these requires children to ensure that both sides are the same. This involves counting the number of counters of a particular colour on both sides of the pattern to make sure they are the same. (Children may spontaneously make symmetrical patterns with construction materials.) Children can also use pegboards divided in half, with half a pattern to copy or complete.

Incidental activities

This is a valuable activity if done by children either at dinner-time or in the home corner. They may do it by putting one plate on one place at a time, but try to encourage children to see that counting offers a quicker and more efficient strategy.

Helping to set up an everyday activity, or preparing for a special party or outing, can offer children opportunities to discuss "How many do we need?" and "Have we got the right number?".

When tidying up, children can check that the number of items matches the label on their container — for instance, on a tin of scissors or a rack of pencils.

Laying the table offers opportuniites for counting.

Outdoor/physical activity

All the physical skill activities can provide opportunities for counting to see how many you can do, and then trying to do more the next time. Try:

- hopping
- skipping
- aiming at skittles
- throwing
- bouncing or catching balls
- scoring goals in football

How many bricks tall is the beanstalk?

How many geraniums do we need to have one in each pot? Two in a pot?

How many pots do we need to plant out these bedding plants one to a pot?

Whole-group activities

Counting children for the register, or to check dinner numbers, provides a clear purpose for counting as well as practice in using larger numbers.

A system where children put a card in a box if they want a school dinner can be used as an opportunity for children to count the cards and inform the cook.

Children can take it in turns to toss a large dice, say the number, then bang the drum that number of times. If they throw a 1 they can have another turn. They could use different instruments, clap or do actions.

Purposes for counting
Activity: Bulbs

Children will experience

◆ using counting in order to compare

◆ using mathematical language: 'the same number', 'more'

◆ using and discussing problem solving strategies

Equipment

◆ bulbs

◆ potting compost

◆ large pots or bowls

Getting started

The problem is to share out the bulbs equally between the pots. You could start with two pots and six bulbs, but the more bulbs you use, the more obvious the need for children to count becomes.

Ask the children, "Can you put the same number of bulbs in each pot?". Observe their strategies and discuss with them how they solved the problem.

Questions to ask the children

Are there the same number of bulbs in each pot?

How do you know?

How many bulbs are in this pot?

And this one?

Which pot has more bulbs than the others?

Have the pots each got the same number of bulbs in them?

How can you make it so that the pots have the same amount of bulbs in each?

Purposes for counting	the children may . . .	if so . . .	In counting generally
	put random amounts into the pots, or move the bulbs randomly from pot to pot	they may not be engaged with the problem, and you will need to rephrase it or put it in a different context, or try again another day	
understanding why we need to count	make sensible estimates by eye, or deal the bulbs out one to each pot in turn until they are all gone, but not actually count them	encourage them to use counting to check that they have the same amount try repeating the task with an odd number, or a larger number of bulbs, so that there is a clearer purpose in counting to check see if they know that counting tells you how many there are, by asking "How many are there?", or "Can you get me five?"	understanding counting the number sequence
	use counting, but get the numbers mixed up or miscount the bulbs	try with smaller numbers or choose some activities from the previous sections	organising counting
counting to compare	use counting, but count all the bulbs together, rather than counting the number in each pot separately count, but not compare the numbers	re-emphasise the need to check there are the same number in each pot, by finding out how many there are in each try some more activities from this section which show the use of counting	understanding counting
	spontaneously use counting to check, and conclude that there are the same or more	if children spontaneously use counting and interpret the results, try bigger numbers, other activities from this section or activities from the 'Number Patterns and Problems' section	number patterns and problems

Representing numbers

Representing numbers

Important aspects of representing numbers

Recognising numerals
◆ *personally significant numbers*
◆ *linking numerals to amounts*

Recording numbers for a purpose
◆ *representing numbers with pictures, tallies or numerals*

Forming numerals
◆ *internalising the shape of numerals and writing them freehand*

Recognising numerals

Children need to recognise that there are many purposes for using numerals (written number symbols):

- as 'labels', such as bus numbers (nominal numbers)
- to indicate an amount (cardinal numbers)
- to identify position in a sequence, for example house numbers or page numbers (ordinal numbers)
- to record measurements

Children often have experience of numerals as labels, for example door numbers or bus numbers. They may also recognise numbers that are of personal significance to them (their age, shoe size, telephone numbe or house number). However, they may not distinguish between numbers used as 'identifiers' (ordinal numbers) and numbers which are used to indicate how many things there are (cardinal numbers). For example, the number 5 on a door does not mean that five people live there, whereas the number 6 marked on an egg box does show the number of eggs inside. It is important to provide contexts in which numbers are used to indicate 'how many':

- reading labels to check that all the parts of a game are in the box (such as four spiders for 'Incy Wincy')
- using numerals in dice games, number jigsaws and computer programs
- reading numerals in books of number rhymes and stories
- reading recipe cards showing numbers of cupfuls or eggs
- reading out the register, or counting aloud the number of children having school dinners each day

Understanding number in the context of measurements can be problematic for young children, since these tend to make use of units which are invisible to the young child (10 kilos, 100 cm or 4 years). As a result the child will not experience numerals indicating an amount, or number of things, unless we provide them with relevant experiences.

It is important for children to experience number in as many contexts as possible. In their day-to-day world, children come across numbers constantly on TV remote controls, microwaves ovens, clocks, calendars, cars and street signs. We need to help them to make sense of these encounters, and to link their experiences at home with what they learn in school.

Have a range of resources available that show numbers, including:

- digital displays and calculators
- wooden and plastic numbers for children to handle
- sandpaper, velvet and other tactile numbers
- numbers on carpet tiles
- number friezes and grids
- calendars and old birthday cards
- clocks and watches

Recording numbers for a purpose

Using numbers to make a record of 'how many there are' helps children appreciate the function of written numbers. However, it is important to encourage children to make these records in their own way. This can give them confidence at a crucial stage of learning (they feel that what they are doing is acceptable, not 'wrong') and it gives us a chance to assess in more detail what they know and understand about numbers. Some children prefer to use tallies, inventing a system of tallying for themselves. (Note that children are tallying when they represent a number by holding up the appropriate number of fingers.)

Some children may know how to write numerals, but not understand exactly how they are used. They may, for example, record two by writing '1 2' and three by writing '1 2 3'. Others will know there should be only one symbol, but not know how to write it.

Children need to become familiar with numerals, and should be able to use plastic and wooden numerals for recording amounts before they start actually writing numerals. Selecting the appropriate numeral on a calculator or computer is another way of recording without writing.

Forming numerals

Forming numerals is an important skill, which may not develop at the same time as children's understanding of how numerals can be used. Children will need experience of handling large tactile numbers, as well as opportunities to form numerals using large movements, with paint and sand as well as pencils and paper. When children are initially learning how to form numerals you will need to advise them on which stroke to do first, and where to go next. Mnemonics can help here; some children find it helpful to chant as they draw the numeral 4, 'Down, along and down'. However, don't worry if children continue to reverse their numerals. Many children do not overcome this until much later.

Patterns

When writing numerals over ten, children can spot patterns at a variety of levels. They may recognise numerals in larger numbers without necessarily knowing how to say them, or identify the '1, 2, 3, 4 …' and '10, 20, 30 …' patterns running across and down a 100-square. For more on number patterns see the next section, 'Number Patterns and Problems'.

These five-year-old children watched the film *A Hundred and One Dalmations*. They drew dalmations and counted the number of spots. Manwi counted 9 spots, and wrote down her total (left); Neil counted also 9, and chose to write the number '101' at the top of his picture as well (right).

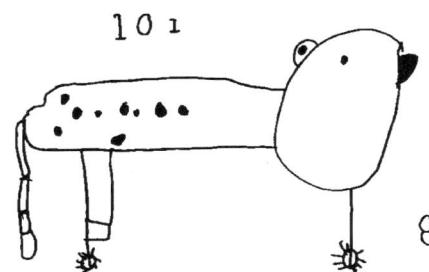

Recognising numerals

Adult-led activities

Dice games

Games using dice marked with numerals rather than spots give children practice in reading numerals and linking them to a number of moves or objects to count. Children in mixed-age groups will usually help each other to recognise numerals, so you could use dice with numerals up to ten. A number frieze on the wall nearby helps as a reference.

Making numbers

Trace a number on the child's back, and let them guess what it is. Children can then trace numbers on each others' backs.

Adults and children can work together making numerals from string, or sandpaper stuck onto card. Can a child hold the number and say what it is with their eyes shut?

Independent play

Lottery numbers

Some children are familiar with lottery numbers. You could provide lottery tickets in the home corner for role play. Numbers written on polystyrene balls and used in a salad spinner can be used for lottery or bingo games.

Interactive display

As mentioned in the 'Understanding Counting' section, children can match illustrations depicting different numbers of things to the appropriate numeral. You could put bags under all the numerals so that children can 'post' the pictures into the right bags.

Role play

Most children will have seen numerals on appliances at home such as TV remote controls, microwave ovens, washing machines and so on. However, many appliances in the home corner at school do not show these numerals. Make your own appliances, with or without the children's help, or adapt the existing ones by painting or sticking on numbers.

Games and apparatus

Many commercial games, such as Bingo or Lotto, and structural apparatus such as Unifix trays or numeral jigsaws, involve matching amounts or pictures to numerals.

Computer games

Games such as 'Animated Number' give children experience of recognising numerals. Children can work together to help and correct each other in matching amounts to numerals.

Calculators

Calculators provide a useful basis for discussion about numbers. Children are usually interested in large numbers on the calculator, and some may know that 100 has two zeros and a million has six. There seems to be little difficulty for children in relating the numerals on a calculator to other numbers, and the simplified way in which a calculator represents 'difficult' numbers like 5 is actually helpful to some children. Calculators can also be used for keeping tallies, by adding '1' each time.

Collage

Children can collect tickets, trade cards, adverts, minicab cards and so on, and make these into a large number collage.

Incidental activities

Talking

Big numbers crop up in conversation and stories, and are exciting to children, although they may not understand exactly what they mean. A number line or square showing numbers up to 100 is useful to refer to during such conversations.

Writing and drawing

If children are looking for ideas, suggest they write all the numbers they know.

Rainy days

Children can collect rain water and read and discuss the numbers on the measuring jug.

Outdoor/physical activities

Number track

A number track painted outside with powder paint provides an excellent opportunity for activities involving the recognition of numerals, and is surprisingly durable (lasting for several weeks). Children can:

- jump along, saying the numbers as they land on them
- throw a bean bag along and then jump to it, saying the number it landed on and how many jumps they made

With numbers over ten, children can say any numerals they recognise within the bigger numbers, while some will attempt to count to higher numbers as they jump.

Number hunt

Hide wooden numbers from 0 to 9 (one of each) and ask children to look for them. They will know they have found them all when they have a complete collection.

Number walk

Children can walk around the school or local area, spotting numerals on signs, cars, doors, shops and so on, and discussing what they are for.

Whole-group activities

Hickety-tickety

Children hold up the number of fingers that corresponds with the numeral shown them by the teacher in this useful rhyme:

Hickety tickety rumpa rickety
Horny cup [hold up number]
How many fingers do you hold up?

Books and songs

Books and songs provide unpressurised opportunities for children to become familiar with numbers. Have large numerals available so that children can select the appropriate one to go with, say, the number of currant buns or frogs left, or the number of toys left in the toy box.

Numerals can also be stuck with Velcro onto felt (useful for 'Ten Green Bottles') and other props, such as puppets or pictures on a magnet board, can be combined with numerals to make their meaning clear.

Magnet boards and felt boards

These provide an inviting variation of matching pictures to numerals.

Number folders

Give each child a folder to store numbers important to them: their phone number, a birthday card with their age on it, or a picture of their family with showing how many people there are. They can also keep in their folder a set of 0–9 number cards for various games.

Recognising numerals
Activity: My number book

Children will experience

◆ talking about numbers that are of personal significance to them

◆ recognising and writing numerals

◆ linking these to a variety of meanings, including amounts

Equipment

◆ paper and fastening or little pre-made books

◆ calculator, box of numerals, number line or chart, numeral stamp

◆ pens for writing and drawing

◆ height chart, weighing scales

Getting started

Talk to the child about the numbers they know. You might prompt them with suggestions such as age, door number, phone number (their own and other people in their family). You may know of family interests from conversations with parents. Occupations like shopkeeping, activities like car journeys or visits to relatives, or interests like DIY may reveal particular experiences with numbers.

Discuss measurements such as height, weight and shoe and clothes sizes. Children could pick the numbers out of a box of wooden numerals, find it on the calculator, or you could show them the numeral. They can then choose some numbers to talk about, or to write about and illustrate in their number book or folder.

Questions to ask the children

You know lots of numbers. Can you tell me the ones you know?

Do you know any songs or rhymes with numbers in?

Do you know your door number?

Can you tell me about your numbers?

Which number tells you how old you are?
How old were you before your last birthday?
Do you know how old you will be on your next birthday?

What size shoes do you wear?
How could you find out?
What size are your clothes?
Can you see the size on the label?

Do you know what those numbers are for?
What do they tell you?

	the children may . . .	**if so . . .**	
recognising numerals	not recognise any numbers	you could show them their age, and door number, as a start	
	not recognise some styles of number	compare different birthday cards and large digital displays, and discuss the different ways of writing numbers such as 4s and 9s	
	have difficulty writing numerals	let them do their best attempt, combined with marks or drawings to show what they mean, or use numeral stamps; and try some other activities	**forming numerals**
	read numerals to ten confidently	ask children to read larger numbers, perhaps arranging wooden numerals to show numbers over ten with the help of a number chart or number line; or try some of the activities in this section for numbers up to 20	**patterns in numerals**

Recording numbers for a purpose

Independent play

The aeroplane; The café

Many imaginative play areas include examples of numerals, and adults can demonstrate the purposes of them. For instance:

- an aeroplane involves tickets, seat numbers, and control dials
- shops and cafés includes menus with prices, prices labels, money and tills
- hairdressers, travel agents and garages include clocks, calendars and appointment books
- hospitals and clinics provide many of the above along with various measuring scales, height charts
- home corners may include videos, digital clocks, timers, washing machines, tape recorders, TVs, magazines and catalogues.

Incidental activities

Cooking

Use simple recipe cards with quantities written as numerals, and ask children to help to work out what needs doing.

As well as in recipes, cooking provides opportunities to read numerals in recipes and on food packets, measuring scales, ovens and timers.

Tidying up

Tidy-up labels provide a clear purpose for linking numerals to amounts. Children can write labels showing how many pairs of scissors there should be in a pot, or how many counters in a game.

Surveys

Making surveys of, for instance, whether more boys than girls are using the trikes, the computer or the construction area can identify the need for a fair turn-taking system. Children can record by keeping a tally or counting and writing numerals. Outside, surveys of minibeasts or traffic provide interesting results for scientific or safety purposes.

How many here?

Children can take turns carrying information (the register, or a number card) to the secretary or cook about the number of children in school today.

A five-year-old produced this piece of writing — including the numbers — without prompting from an adult. When asked what the story was, he said "The dragon is going to kill all the people".

Opportunities for talking about numbers as labels, numbers showing the amount, and numbers used for measures

Outdoor/physical activities

A number walk

This involves spotting numerals in different contexts and discussing what they mean. For instance, the numbers on a bus might indicate vehicle registration, depot number and capacity as well as its route. Taking photos of a range of signs in the area also provides a talking point back in the classroom.

Scoring

When children are playing skittles, provide them with a chalk board or an easel and paper and encourage them to write their names and record their scores. They may use their own marks, or write in numerals.

They could also keep score when:

- seeing how many bean bags they can put in a bucket
- counting their skipping record
- doing circuits of an obstacle course.

For reference, you could provide a box of numerals, a calculator, and a number chart or number line.

Whole group activities

A number wall

Children can record numbers they know on a number wall. These might include their house numbers, car numbers, or the ages of people in their families, and could be accompanied by pictures. The number wall can provide a good introduction to large numbers. Photos taken on a number walk could be used as part of the display.

Calendars and clocks

Draw children's attention to times and dates when interesting things are happening. This provides valuable experience of larger numerals used for a specific purpose. Children will probably relate this to conversations at home about bedtimes or birthdays. Advent calendars are interesting to make for counting how many days to Christmas: use ordinary calendars in the same way for other events or festivals. For example, make an 'advent calendar' for counting down to the likely hatching date for the chicks or butterflies.

Some children enjoy drawing sets of nesting shapes, and counting how many they can fit inside the original shape.

Edward made certain he had counted every shape by putting a blob on each one, then numbering each blob.

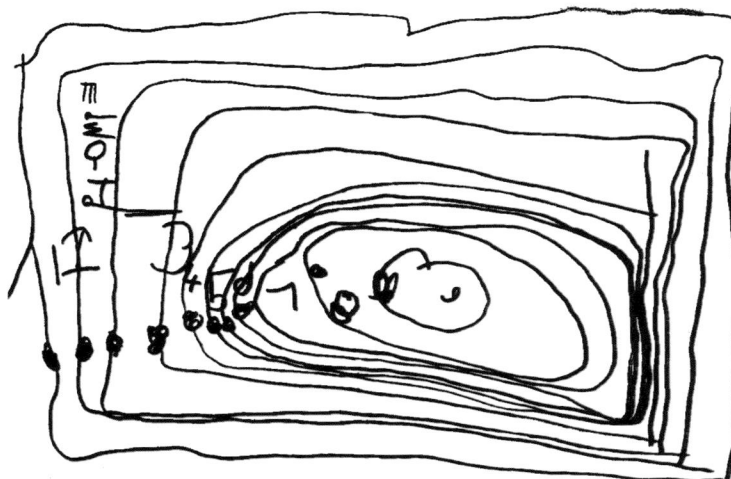

Written numbers for a purpose
Activity: Bears in boxes

Children will experience

◆ representing numbers for a purpose

◆ devising their own system of recording (or using numerals)

◆ reading their own system of recording (or numerals) with a clear purpose

Equipment

◆ some tins, boxes or pots, preferably with lids

◆ small, attractive identical items, like tiny cubes or plastic bears

◆ Post-it notes and pens

Getting started

Put a different number of bears in each box, from zero to four. Ask the children to guess how many are in each by shaking the boxes, and then to check by counting.

Next, mix the boxes up and challenge the children to pick out a box containing two bears. After they have tried this a few times, for different numbers of bears, suggest putting labels on the boxes to help them remember how many are in each box. Ask them to count how many are in the box first, but leave it up to them to decide how to mark the label.

Play the game again and see if the children can read their labels.

As an extension, ask them to shut their eyes while you take one bear out, and challenge them to find which box it has come from.

Questions to ask the children

Can you put something on the label which will help us to remember how many there are? Just do it any way you like.

What you are going to put on that label?

Can you put some marks on the label to help us remember?

What does that label say?

How many are there in the box?

How many should be in that box?

What to look for . . .

the children may . . .	if so . . .
make random marks which they cannot read back	check that they know how many are in the boxes; if they have trouble counting, refer to the previous section
make pictures of things in the box	provide them with numerals and suggest they use them to label the boxes
keep some kind of tally, marking once for each object in the box	this shows that they appreciate the number, but need more familiarity with numerals and their use in indicating an amount
write numerals, but write '12' for two or '123' for three	as before, they need more experience of the function of numerals in labelling amounts
write numerals, or approximations to them	children may know numerals, but not yet be able to form them properly, in which case they need plenty of practice (see the 'Recognising and Writing Numerals' section); try the activity using larger numbers if children are using written numerals accurately for the numbers from one to four

written numbers for a purpose

understanding counting

linking numerals to amounts

forming numerals

Forming numerals

Adult-led activities

Board game

Children can make a track game based on a topic of interest (going to the park, shopping, or a trip to the seaside). Help them to write the numbers on the track, and to collect other necessary equipment.

Number plates

Get children to look at the number plates on staff cars, then make their own number plates for the trikes. They could make other signs related to trike use — for instance, numbering the parking bays to match the trike number plates.

Open-ended record sheets

Make record sheets with a large oval drawn on them and all the numbers listed underneath. Children draw the objects (for example, the conkers they collected) in the oval, and choose the appropriate number to write on their picture.

Cooking numbers

Handling large numbers allows children to form an image of the characteristics of each numeral. Making numbers out of playdough provides an opportunity to discuss the difference between, say, 2 and 5, or 6 and 9.

The bean game

Children can use a resource sheet like the one illustrated below to play the bean game:

Paint nine flat beans on one side only. Children toss the beans and count how many land coloured side up, then write that number in the appropriate column. The first person to get the same number three times is the winner.

1	2	3	4	5	6	7	8	9

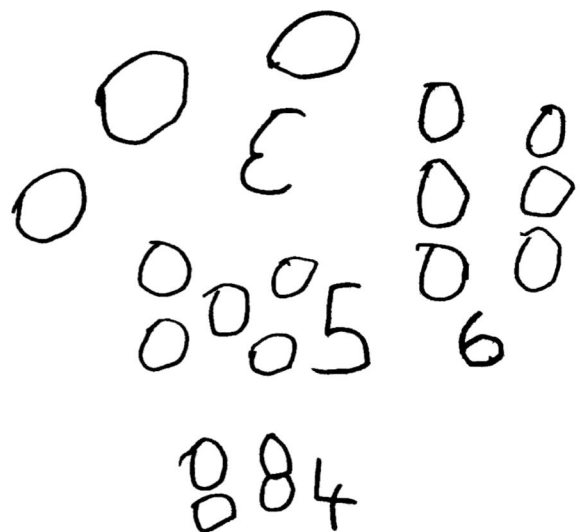

Faizal copied the spots on a dice, then wrote numbers to go with them.

Opportunities for internalising the shape of numerals and writing them freehand

Incidental activity

Calendars

Hang an old calendar on the wall so that children can copy the numbers in clay, Plasticine, or in the sand tray. Leave sheets of squared paper near the calendar so that children can copy the numbers, one to a square.

Independent play

Making machines

Children can help you to make machines that show numbers using large cardboard boxes: you could make a telephone booth, a washing machine, a microwave, a petrol pump, or a photocopier.

Role play

Children can make bus, aeroplane or cinema tickets, showing the price. They could also make the numbered tickets that show whose turn it is at the deli counter.

They can write menus and price lists for a café or shop.

They can make an appointment book for the garage, the hairdresser or the doctor, and write times in it — or write names and numbers to indicate who is first, second, third and so on.

Making cards

Children can make birthday cards, or party invitations, for real situations as well as pretend ones. Help them to write the age, date, time, and other numbers they might need.

Outdoor/physical activities

Scoring

Set up an easel with a large sheet of paper, or section a chalkboard with columns for names and scores. Children might want to keep scores when:

- playing skittles
- seeing how many bean bags they can put in a bucket
- counting their skipping record
- doing circuits of an obstacle course

Painting

Children can write or paint large numbers in chalk or water on the playground or walls, or using paint on paper.

Whole group activity

Television

Look at short clips from programmes such as Number Time or Sesame Street to see how numbers are formed.

Sammi wrote the sequence of numbers 1 to 17 on the border of his picture.

Forming numerals
Activity: Birthday cards

Children will experience

◆ representing numbers

◆ forming numerals

◆ using numbers in different contexts

Equipment

◆ card

◆ paper

◆ felt-tipped pens

◆ glue

◆ fabric and card scraps

Getting started

Children make birthday cards, badges or party invitations.

If they are making birthday cards, they can make them either for dolls and toys, or for each other, whether or not they have imminent birthdays. This will mean they need to make cards showing ages such as $4\frac{1}{4}$ or $4\frac{1}{2}$.

If they are making party invitations, encourage them to write any numbers that are appropriate: the date and time of the party, the telephone number to respond to, the door number in the street where the party is, and so on.

Questions to ask the children

How old are you?

What number was on your card?

How many candles do you have on your cake?

What are these numbers on the party invitation for?

Where does it tell you what time to come?

Where does it tell you what house number you need to go to?

Forming numerals

Representing numbers generally

forming numerals

understanding counting

the children may . . .	if so . . .
write letters rather than numerals	check that they understand what numerals are
not know how to write a number	offer examples for them to look at and copy; give verbal directions
write the same number over and over again	draw attention to other numbers they know; give them more experience of looking at numbers in a range of contexts
write some recognisable bits of numbers, but miss out, say, the cross on the 4	offer examples for them to look at and copy; give verbal directions
write some numbers like letters, for example, write 1 as i	don't worry, but discuss with the children what they are doing and show them some examples
write some numbers back to front, for example, draw a 2 instead of 5	discuss starting from the top; develop chants and mnemonics for correct number formation
form letters in the wrong direction, for example, start from the bottom	do some activities in a group where numbers are shown upside down or back to front, and ask the children to spot the mistakes

Number patterns and problems

Number patterns and problems

Important aspects of representing numbers

Patterns in number
- *repeating patterns*
- *relationships such as 'one more than'*

Estimating
- *visual patterns*
- *thinking about relative sizes*

Comparing
- *estimating*
- *pairing*
- *counting*

Addition and subtraction
- *adding one or two*
- *working on 'hidden number' problems in various ways*
- *partitioning*

Multiplication, division, fractions
- *working with pairs*
- *sharing*

Engaging with pattern

Many adults give a hollow laugh when they hear about how fascinating number patterns are — this was not the experience of their own education. It is also commonly thought that early mathematical experience should be about the usefulness of numbers, and that the early stages do not afford opportunities to appreciate number patterns for their own sake. However, there are patterns in number which young children will spontaneously comment on, represent and appreciate. Some of the repeating number patterns that children need to recognise in order to say and write the numbers up to 20, 30 or beyond have

already been mentioned. There are other patterns involving mathematical relationships which children can spot and use: the 'one more than' pattern is an example. It may not be obvious to small children that the next number in the counting sequence is always worth one more than the previous number. But knowing this relationship is useful when adding one (or two), because children can simply say the next number (or the next number but one).

Most children engage with the 'one more' pattern through number rhymes. The relationship can be demonstrated visually by making 'staircase' patterns with cubes or other objects, going up in ones. You can also use cubes to make repeating patterns such as '3, 2, 3, 2', or '1, 2, 3, 1, 2, 3'.

Harder for children to understand are patterns represented by numbers above ten. In numbers such as 12, 15 or 18 the '1' represents ten; in a number such as 23 the '2' represents two tens, and so on. This pattern can be appreciated visually in a 100-square, and verbally when children learn to say numbers over 20. Familiarity with these visual and verbal patterns forms a foundation for later understanding of the value of the digits, or 'place value'.

Visual patterns

Many very young children can recognise amounts like two or three at a glance, and will soon learn the patterns for four, five and six as shown on dice. They will also learn to recognise and represent these numbers with their fingers. This recognition at a glance of a number of things is called 'subitising', and is useful for recognising small numbers within bigger numbers. For instance, some four-year-olds will comment on the 'doubles': four being made up of two twos, six being two threes, and so on. The visual and verbal pattern of 'two and two is four' and the symmetry of representing this with fingers or dots appeals to the young child's sense of pattern, which will later develop into an understanding of the multiplication and division relationships of doubling and halving.

It is helpful for young children to become familiar with the ways in which a number can be split up into two or three smaller ones, using fingers, objects or pictures. For instance, 6 can be split into 3 and 3, or 2 and 2 and 2, or 5 and 1. An understanding of this helps later on with the number bonds that are essential for solving addition and subtraction problems. Encourage children to see numbers like 6 as 'one hand and one finger', or 5 and 1.

The sizes of numbers

Children need to develop a feel for the relative sizes of numbers, and to understand which numbers are bigger than others. For instance: "Would you rather have 7 sweets or 9 sweets?" Questions such as this require knowledge of the increasing value of numbers in the counting sequence, and some experience of handling numbers of things and of comparing amounts.

Comparison of number sizes gets more difficult with large numbers, as any adult who has suffered young children guessing their age will know. Activities such as guessing how many things are in the jar, which involve estimation, are fun for young children, and involve an important aspect of numeracy. Arranging numbers in order according to a number line helps children to see which numbers come before others, and how far apart they are.

Comparing

Comparing the numbers of things in two sets can be done by a variety of methods: subitising (the recognition of small amounts at a glance); estimating; pairing one to one; or counting. You may need to convince young children who are lacking in confidence that counting works, since they may continue to maintain that one set is larger than another even after they have counted them and found them to have the same number. Adults need to discuss what the counting shows: "The last number you say tells you how many there are".

Very young children will not know how to use counting as a means for comparison. Rather than counting the two sets separately and comparing the numbers ("1 2 3 4, 1 2 3 4 … They are the same"), they may tend to carry on counting from one set to another ("1 2 3 4 5 6 7 8"). You will need to explain to the children the different purposes for counting, and introduce contexts in which the purpose for comparing is made clear.

Addition and subtraction

Young children first learn about adding or subtracting one or two in the context of games, rhymes and stories. However, children of three and four rarely have any general understanding of addition, subtraction or equivalence relationships, and so cannot really understand what '+', '−' and '=' signs stand for (although '+' may be used as shorthand for 'and').

Children may meet these signs when playing schools with older siblings, or playing with the calculator, computer or on TV volume controls, but it is unnecessary at this stage to emphasise these symbols, or to use equations of the form '3 + 2 = 5', until they are older and have a wider experience. Some people argue that we should introduce '=' by emphasising the idea of equivalence in a variety of equation forms, such as '5 = 4 + 1' and '2 + 3 = 4 + 1'. Reading '=' as 'makes' is unhelpful. The SCAA document *Desirable Outcomes for Children's Learning on Entering Compulsory Education* emphasises the importance of the language used in solving practical addition and subtraction problems. Written 'sums' are generally considered inappropriate for children of this age.

However, for children who show confidence in dealing with small numbers, simple and practical number problems are definitely a good idea. Children can begin to solve 'hidden number'problems, for example, where they count a handful of beans, some of which are then hidden, and guess how many have been taken away. Mental strategies to work out the hidden number might include visualising, using fingers or 'counting on'. Using fingers as a counting tool is an age-old strategy that can be very useful in helping young children to become familiar with all sorts of number facts, such as seeing that 4 fingers can be made up of 3 on one hand and 1 on the other, or 2 and 2, or 4 and 0.

Whatever problems children begin to tackle, there will be opportunities to discuss predictions, methods and explanations, all of which require children to use logical strategies and mathematical skills for a purpose.

Multiplication, division and fractions

Counting Pairs

Multiplication can be difficult for young children. Counting two or more objects as a unit is an important mathematical skill, and experience of pairs will help to familiarise children with the idea of counting in groups. Help them to come to terms with the idea of treating two things as an item by talking about pairs of shoes, gloves, eyes, and so on.

Pelmanism is particularly good for demonstrating the value of pairs: encourage children to count their pairs and their total number of cards.

Sharing

Children can actively participate in sharing either by doling out 'fair shares' by eye (estimating), or more accurately by dealing 'one to you, one to you' and so on. When dealing things out children will sometimes notice that there are, say, 'two threes', and comment on this.

When sharing things out in this way, there will sometimes be a remainder. Children may suggest that the problem can be solved by adding or subtracting ("Give me another one then there's enough"), or by halving ("If I break that in two there'll be enough").

This latter solution shows an early use of fractions ("Half for me and half for you"). Experience with fractions can be arranged by asking children to share out food or playdough. The emphasis should be on equal parts — it is not good enough to have one 'large half' and one 'small half'. It is important here that adults use language precisely, because otherwise children might develop the idea that you can divide a lump of dough into several 'halves'!

'Half' can be used to describe many situations: not just single objects or amounts, but liquids, shapes, weights and lengths. Halving can involve numbers as well as single items, as children will discover when they learn that 'half of four is two'. This will be far easier for children to understand if they are familiar with the idea of doubling (which is the inverse operation).

Children also experience fractions when their older siblings talk about ages such as 'eight and a half'. You can explain this using a number line, showing the place that is halfway between the 8 and the 9. (For this purpose a line is better than a track, as 'halfway' has a much clearer meaning for children when demonstrated on a line.)

Some children may want to know how to write $\frac{1}{2}$, perhaps in order to write their age, but for most children it will remain a meaningless symbol for some time to come.

When using a keyboard, children will come across the '+' and '=' symbols, and may well ask what they mean.

Patterns in number

Adult-led activities

Print and stamp

Once children can hold the idea of a pattern such as 'red, blue, red, blue', they can begin to make other simple number patterns using different media, such as

- printing and stamping numerals in patterns such as '1, 2, 1, 2, 1, 2' or '1, 2, 3, 1, 2, 3'
- using bricks or beads, such as: '1 red bead, 2 blue beads, 3 yellow beads, 1 red bead, 2 blue beads, 3 yellow beads'

Initially, children can continue a sequence you have started, and make their own number patterns later.

Board games

Children can help make a simple board game involving a number track. Ask them to colour alternate squares with different colours according to a pattern, such as 'red, blue, red, blue …'

Talk with the children about the pattern of coloured numbers. Can they shut their eyes and tell you what colour the 2 is? Or the 5?

Playing board games provides opportunities to comment on simple patterns.

Independent play

Numbers over 9

Children can try to record the sequence of numbers over nine by printing, stamping or arranging numerals (you will need plenty of them!), as well as by writing. They will need number charts for reference.

Numbers pegged onto a washing line, or arranged on a felt or magnet board, can be used for 'missing number' or 'mixed-up number' games.

Number jigsaw

Provide some photocopied 100-square jigsaws stuck onto card. Divide them very simply. for instance into rows. Start by just going up to 50.

1	2	3	4	5	6	7	8	9	10
11	12	13	14	15	16	17	18	19	20
21	22	23	24	25	26	27	28	29	30

You could also provide grids and number lines which are either partially filled in or empty, for children to write or print numbers in.

1		3		5
6	7		9	10

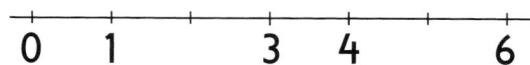

0   1   3   4   6

Incidental activity

Spotting numbers

Two-digit numbers in the children's immediate environment, such as the date on the calendar, door numbers, or the number of children in the class, can be linked to numbers on a number line or number square. These numbers can be displayed in matching styles and sizes. Carpet tile numerals can provide an interesting variation.

This activity can be linked to the number walk and number folder activities on page 25.

Whole group activities

What's the next number?

Try calling out numbers between 10 and 20, and see whether the children can predict the next number, using a chart or number line. You could also use a calculator to demonstrate this pattern. (Most calculators with a constant facility will keep adding 1 if you press

$$\boxed{+}\ \boxed{1}\ \boxed{=}$$

then keep pressing $\boxed{=}$.)

Write down some numbers in sequence, such as 16, 17, 18, and ask children to predict where the next one will go. Counting in patterns, such as 5s or 10s, is a more challenging variation.

Children can also count in twos for rhymes such as 'Ten Green Bottles'.

Counting ears

Count how many ears/eyes/feet/fingers there are in the group. This gives valuable practice in counting in twos, fives or tens.

Chanting

Vary the usual number sequence (one, two, three, four …) by counting in twos (two, four, six …)

Chanting numbers with the whole class.

Patterns in number

Children will experience

- using their knowledge of numbers and numerals
- spotting patterns
- describing patterns

Equipment

- a large 100-square mat or grid with pockets (or one going up to 50)
- a large 1–6 dice

Getting started

A large 100-square, used either inside or outside, provides children with opportunities to notice features such as:

— the same numerals appearing in lots of places

— the same numeral being repeated down a whole column of numbers

— the '1 2 3 4 5 6 7 8 9' pattern being repeated in each row

— the '10 20 30' pattern in the columns

Ask children to count aloud the numbers to 100.

When they have finished, suggest that they play a game in which they throw a dice and jump onto any square containing that number. Later, cover up a number and ask them to describe it, even if they are unable to name it.

Questions to ask the children

> Do you know any numbers here?

> Can you see any numbers that are the same ?

> Can you see your age? Your shoe size? Your door number? Your birthday?

> Can you see any patterns, or numbers repeated lots of times?

> Can you say all the numbers going along a row? Or down a line or column? What comes after 29? 39? 49?

> I'm going to cover up one of the numbers. Can you tell me what it is? Or what it looks like? How do you know?

What to look for . . .

	the children may . . .	if so . . .	
	comment on any number, or any two numbers the same	see if they can say any more about them, or think of anywhere nearby where they can be found	**representing numbers**
repeating patterns	spot some patterns, such as: • numbers starting with the same digit along the rows • numbers ending with the same digit down the columns • numbers going '1, 2, 3, 4, 5, 6, 7, 8, 9' along the rows and down the columns	discuss these and ask other children for more ideas, but leave some patterns still to be found	
relationships such as 'one more than'	ask questions such as • "Why is 11 next to one?" • "Where is zero?" • "Why does it go '7, 8, 9, 0' at the end?"	encourage these questions and repeat and discuss them with the whole group to encourage other children to voice questions; explain as simply and clearly as you can	
	count along but get stuck early on	draw their attention to ways in which the verbal patterns are linked to the written patterns; encourage children to count a little further each time	**number sequence**
	get stuck at 29, or say 'twenty-ten'	point out the '20, 30, 40, 50' pattern, and practise saying it, then combine it with the 'umpty-one, umpty-two' pattern; finally, repeat the '29, 30, 31, … 39, 40, 41, … 49, 50, …' pattern	
relationships such as 'ten and …'	count all the way to 100 and recognise all the numbers identify hidden numbers	see if they can: • write 2-digit numbers read out by you • count or write numbers over 100 • count in other languages • count out a given number of things • count forward and backwards from different starting points	**understanding counting**

Estimating
Opportunities

Adult-led activities

Handfuls

Place a collection of objects such as beans, conkers, buttons or 'jewels' on a tray, and ask each child to take a handful. Ask "Whose hand do you think can hold the most? ... How can we find out?".

Jewels

Put out a collection of 'jewels' and ask the children "Which colour do you think there are most of? ... How can we find out?".

Board games

Ask the children "How many more jumps do you need to make before you reach 'home'?"; "How many pieces are there on the board?".

Dice games

Use dice on which the spots are arranged in an unusual pattern to play various dice games. Alternatively, use dice with more than six spots, arranged in some sort of pattern.

One very simple dice game is 'Nice Things', which is played as follows:

- Children have 10 (or 20) conkers, beads, animals, or toy cars each

- They take turns to toss the dice, say the number, and pass that many of their objects to the person on their left

- The dice is passed round to the right, to ensure that, as soon as a child has given away some of their treasure, they are given some more by their neighbour.

Independent play

Design and technology

Encourage children to estimate how many items they will need to make whatever they are planning — for example: "How many pages do you need for your book?"; "How many wheels on your truck?".

Tea parties

Ask questions such as "How many dolls are there at your party?" "How many chairs will you need?" Accept either approximate answers or accurate ones where children count before responding. Help children to distinguish between the two by the wording of your response: "Yes, there are about five dolls" or "You've counted five dolls".

Incidental activity

How many do we need?

Preparations of all kinds, such as setting up an activity, or preparing food and drinks for a party or picnic (whether real or imaginary), require estimations. Involve children in guessing the number and counting to see whether the number looks right, and to check it exactly.

Outdoor activity

Counting

Ask "How many children do you think are on the climbing frame?" "About how many more are there on the frame than on the train?" "How many children are wearing hats?". Children may give you an approximate answer, or count before responding. Affirm what children are doing by responding accordingly: "Yes, there are about seven children on the frame" or "There are five people with hats, and you know because you counted them".

How many children can go on the hammock?

Whole-group activities

Books

Picture books provide many opportunities for children to guess how many things are pictured on a page, and then count them to check.

Hot dot spotters

Briefly show children a number of things arranged in a pattern. These might be:

- objects on a magnet or felt board
- toys under a cloth
- flashcards
- spots on large dice or giant cards or dominoes

Allow just a second or two for children to see how many things there are, then cover them with a cloth. Ask the children to hold up their fingers to indicate how many things they think they saw. If they have numeral folders, they can hold up numerals.

If there are five or fewer objects, arrange them in different ways so that children learn to recognise small numbers of things even when they are randomly organised.

If using more than five objects, ensure that they are arranged to form groups, since children find it very difficult to recognise numbers above five at a glance if they are randomly organised. The skill of 'seeing how many' without counting is called 'subitising'.

Number cards

Give each children a set of 1–5 number cards. When playing Peek-a-Boo, ask children to indicate their guess by holding up the appropriate card.

Estimating

Children will experience

◆ estimating

◆ using their knowledge of numbers

◆ comparing numbers

Equipment

◆ jar containing a collection of objects that are of interest to the children — to be changed daily

◆ paper for children to record estimates

◆ number line for reference

Getting started

This activity is for use with either a large or small group of children. Put a small number of objects into a jar (such as four small furry teddies, or six tennis balls), and ask children how many they think there are. Children record their guesses under their names on a record sheet, and then the objects are taken out and counted. As an alternative to recording their guesses on paper, children could peg name cards next to their chosen numbers on a number line.

If the jar is available to the children throughout the day, but not opened for counting until the end of the day, this will give each child a better chance to estimate and count the contents of the jar in his or her own time and without pressure. As individual children gain confidence, you can challenge them to estimate larger numbers of things.

Questions to ask the children

Can you show on your fingers how many you think are in the jar?

Do you think there are more than three?

Are there more or fewer than in yesterday's jar?

Is it about five, or about ten?
Can you pick the number on the number line you think it could be?

Do you know what those numbers are for?
What do they tell you?

Can you record your estimate?
Can you find your number on the number line?

What to look for . . .

	the children may . . .	if so . . .	
	make wild guesses, even for very small numbers	give them more experience of counting small numbers (see the 'Counting' section); try revealing small numbers of things on a magnet board for a few seconds	understanding counting
visual patterns	know immediately by looking how many objects there are, with 2, 3 or 4 objects	the children may recognise the visual pattern of the numbers: try increasing the number, but still arranging the objects in small groups, so that children can see that eight, for example, is made up of four and four	
	make wild guesses for numbers from five to ten	encourage children to count numbers over five on their fingers, so that they begin to see that seven, for instance, is one whole hand and two fingers, or 'five and two more', as well as recognising doubles (6 as 3 + 3, 8 as 4 + 4, and so on)	addition and subtraction
		relate numbers to sequences familiar to the child, such as pictures or friezes	
	make reasonable guesses, such as whether a number is larger or smaller than the one before it	refine the estimate by increasing or reducing by 2 or 3	
relative sizes	estimate accurately to within one or two	increase the numbers involved	

Comparing
Opportunities

Adult-led activities

Handfuls

Children can grab two handfuls of beans, acorns, buttons or nuts, and compare by counting which hand can hold the most.

Nice things

You need: small objects such as buttons, shells, beads, building blocks, pieces of fabric and miniature toys; a dice showing one spot, two spots and three spots, twice each; and a saucer for each child. Children collect some objects and place them in their saucer. They take turns to toss the dice, say the number, and then give that many of their things to the child on their left. As the game progresses, discuss who has more objects then their neighbour, who has fewest, and so on.

As a variation, suggest: "When you toss the dice, your neighbour can say which of your nice things they want".

Sand and water

Play 'Nice Things', but instead of a saucer of little objects, each person has a bucket of sand or water and an empty yoghurt pot. They toss the dice, and pass on that many pots full of sand or water to their neighbour.

Bricks

Play 'Nice Things' using building bricks arranged as a tower or wall instead of nice things. Draw children's attention to the changes in the tower's height as the game progresses.

Independent play/Incidental activities

Which holds most?

Compare which teapot will give most cups of tea, or which bottle holds the most drinks.

Sand and water play

Test the capacity of buckets and boats by counting how many cupfuls of liquid, or small objects, they can hold.

Other ideas

Encourage children to make comparisons when balancing scales, or during scientific activities such as testing the strength of different bridges.

Using a bucket for the 'Sand and Water' version of 'Nice Things'.

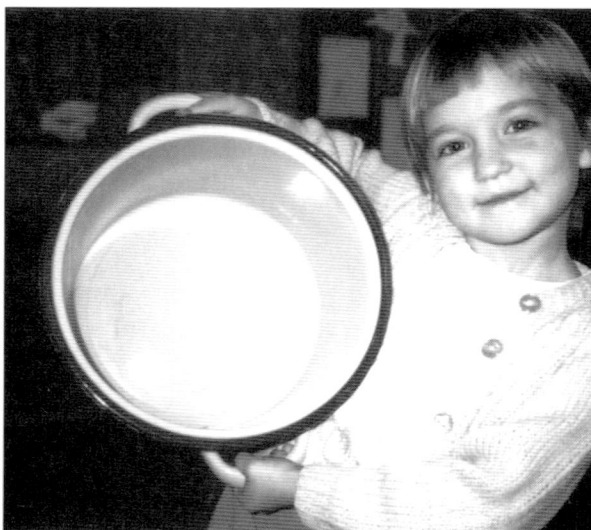

Outdoor activity

Scoring

Scoring to 'improve your best', as mentioned in the 'Representing Numbers' section, gives children an incentive to compare numbers in different ways, by counting and tallying.

Hide and seek

Hide conkers, toy people or feathers in various locations outside. Get children to find them and compare: "Who has most?"; "Has Lisa got more than Mark?". Or hide just a few things, and tell children how many you have hidden. As they find them, discuss with them how many more there are to find.

You could make the hunt topical — say, looking for eggs at Easter time, or triangles when you have been doing work on shapes.

Gardening

Ask "How many bulbs are in that pot?"; "Are there the same number in this pot and that one?"; "Which bulbs are there most of?"

Comparisons occur in other gardening contexts such as comparing runner bean heights, or discovering in which compost trays most seeds came up.

Whole-group activity

Graphs

Make a block graph or pictogram showing data relating to topics of interest such as: 'Our favourite names for the new gerbil' or 'How many teeth we have got'. Discuss the graphs with the children:

"Which name got the most votes?"; "Who has got 15 teeth?"; "How many people chose the name 'Ginger Spice'?"

Unfair shares

Stories such as *The Doorbell Rang*, which involves sharing, give opportunities for you to demonstrate sharing things unfairly, and making comparisons in order to share equally.

Cooking and other sharing situations also give opportunities for discussion of 'unfair sharing' problems.

"How many round things can you find?"

Comparing
Activity: Voting

Children will experience

- counting for a purpose
- comparing numbers and using comparative language
- interpreting and constructing simple graphs in 'real' or symbolic form
- using numerals for a purpose

Equipment

- name cards
- labelled chart with two columns and large spaces to fit name cards
- numerals to attach to chart
- number line for reference

Getting started

Sometimes an obvious opportunity for voting will present itself, such as naming a class pet, but children can also vote on everyday group decisions, such as what kind of biscuit to cook, what games to play at a party, or what story or song to have at group time.

It is best to start with only two choices (move on to three at a later stage). Children can record choices physically, by grouping themselves, and getting into lines which can be paired and compared.

Choices can also be represented with name cards, pictures or tallies on a chart, or by placing cubes in towers. Summarise decisions using numerals on a chart.

Questions to ask the children

How shall we decide?

Which would you rather do?

Which other people agree with you?
Which group do you need to stand in?

How many are there in each group?
What does that mean?

How could we write down how many of each there are?
How else could we do it?

What does that record mean?
How do we make sure everyone has a vote?

What to look for . . .

Comparing			Patterns and problems generally
	the children may . . .	**if so . . .**	
	not have any idea what to do	you will need to provide children with a clear and simplified model of how voting works	
comparing by estimating	say that a shorter bunched-up line of children has fewer than a long spread-out line, because it looks smaller visually	demonstrate that they will need to use pairing and counting in order to establish which line has more	understanding counting for a purpose
comparing by pairing	not compare numbers when lines are paired	the children may need more experience with comparing groups of objects, perhaps in a game situation	
comparing by counting	count groups accurately, but then disregard their counted totals in favour of line length	relate size of numbers to their sequence on the number line do more activities from the 'Understanding Counting' and 'Counting for a Purpose' sections	relative sizes

Addition and subtraction

Adult-led activity/Independent play

Shopping

This can involve adding and subtracting small amounts. Give children a purse with three pennies and price items in the 'shop' at one, two or three pence. Encourage them to consider number combinations for three different items.

Board games; Computer games

Games often involve taking or winning a number of objects according to the throw of a dice. When collecting objects, children can count the new total after two turns. See if they are able to adjust a miscounted number by taking one away from five when there should have been four, or adding one to five when there should have been six.

Similarly, computer games such as 'Animated Number' involve adjusting numbers of objects on screen to match a given number, by adding or subtracting.

Games can be extended by using two dice together.

Café

A group of children place their order at the café — for example, a coke and a bun, a coke and a cheese sandwich, milk and fish fingers, or orange juice and a bun. The child playing the waiter works out how many of each item is required.

Partitioning 1

Children investigate how many different ways a number of objects can be divided into two groups. For example, in how many different ways could:

- five biscuit be arranged on two plates?
- seven play people be shared between two cars?
- eight ten pences be spent on two toys?
- six fingers be shown on two hands?

Partitioning 2

Children investigate problems such as the following:

There are two different kinds of biscuit: jammy dodgers and ginger nuts. You can pick five biscuits altogether. What are the different choices you could make?

Other problems of this kind involve two kinds of things: two different-coloured cubes; horses and cows in a field, and so on.

Board games offer plenty of opportunities for working with numbers.

Incidental/Outdoor activities

How many more: graphing

Surveying activities give rise to the question, "How many more?". This gives rise to the opportunity to introduce the comparative aspect of subtraction called 'finding the difference'.

Scoring with calculators

Some children may already be familiar with calculators, perhaps from their use at home by older siblings, and will be able to use them to keep scores.

Hide and seek

Hide objects in various locations outside. Get children to find them and compare: who has the most. Or hide just a few things, and tell children how many you have hidden. As they find them, discuss with them how many more there are to find.

Tallying with calculators

When surveying traffic, children can keep a tally of the cars they see by pressing (+) (1) and then (=) on a calculator for each car seen.

'Hide and Seek'.

Whole group activities

Stories

Stories (either made up by the teacher or children, or well-known ones such as 'The Shopping Basket') can pose addition and subtraction questions. These can be represented on a magnet board, or children can act out the stories themselves. For example: "The farmer went to market and bought two cows, three pigs and a horse ...".

Imagine

Young children enjoy shutting their eyes and adding objects such as two more bears in their imagination. They can then hold their fingers up to show what they think the total should be.

Number games

Games such as 'Yoghurt Pots' (overleaf) can be played with a large group if the box and counters are big enough. Vary the numbers to suit everyone in the group.

You can change the 'Yoghurt Pots' activity by using other objects, for instance, bugs (made from pebbles) in a box, or teddies hiding behind a chair.

Break a stick of four cubes in half behind your back. Show the children one half, and ask them to guess how many are still hidden.

Addition and subtraction

Activity: Yoghurt pots

Children will experience

- adding one or two
- visualising
- representing numbers on their fingers
- using knowledge of number relationships

Equipment

- an open pot or box
- some identical counters, such as plastic cubes or bears
- optional: a set of plastic or card numbers for each child

Getting started

Put three counters in the pot, counting aloud as you do it to make sure the children know how many are there. Turn the pot upside down, taking one counter out as you do it. Make sure that the children cannot see how many are left underneath.

Now ask them to tell you how many counters are still under the pot. You might put the one removed on top of the pot. Children can show their guesses with fingers, which reduces the noise of 'shouting out', and allows you to scan their responses. If they each have their own set of numerals, they can hold up the number they think it is.

Questions to ask the children

Can you show with your fingers how many we had to start with?

How many do you think are under there now?

Can you show me?

How do you know?

What makes you think that?

How did you work it out?

How many shall we put under there now?

How many shall we take away this time?

I'm going to take two counters away ...

How many do you think are under there now?

Now I'm going to add a counter ...

How many do you think are under there now?

What to look for . . .

Addition and subtraction	the children may . . .	if so . . .	Patterns and problems generally
	repeat the number you started with, or the number you took away	check they know what you are asking: rephrase the activity do some small number activities from the 'Counting' section	understanding counting
	say a number larger (if you subtracted) or smaller (if you added)	do some activities from the 'Estimating' section	estimating
visualising	seem to be relying on imagining small numbers	suggest other strategies, such as adding on one or two at a time play more games and rhymes that involve saying the next number in a sequence	
adding one or two	say the answer correctly when adding one more	try putting bigger numbers in the pot, or adding two	
	say the answer correctly when removing one	try the activity using bigger numbers, or taking away two	
using fingers	not show an answer on their fingers	practise finger representations in another context, but remember that they may not be working it out on their fingers at all; teach children to hold up their fingers systematically, counting 1 on the little finger, 2 on the next finger, 3 on the middle finger and so on	representing numbers
counting on	seem to be relying on counting on large numbers, for example, mentally counting on five from eight	impressive, but encourage them to use number facts, like 'ways of making ten'	
number bonds	explain by saying things like, "Because two and two are four"	explore what other number bonds they know, building on the pattern of doubling numbers in finger play	

Multiplication, division, fractions
Opportunities

Adult-led activities

Pairs (or Pelmanism)

When playing games which involve matching pairs of cards, encourage children to count their cards in twos at the end of the game: "two, four, six". They can also count the pairs: "one, two, three pairs". This can help them to make the appropriate links — four pairs is the same as eight cards, six pairs is twelve cards, and so on.

Sharing

Any precious items, such as 'jewels', sticky shapes, grapes, can be shared between the children so that the sharing out is 'fair'. Discuss what to do if some are left over.

Dice games

Play games using dice, such as games in which children move play people along a track. Take particular note when the child throws a double: see if children can remember what the double is worth by asking "Double three; what's that worth? … Yes, six".

Independent play

Pretend cooking

Playing with dough and having tea parties in the home corner both involve problems of dividing and sharing.

Sharing

When sharing biscuits, toys or Plasticine 'sweets' between children or dolls, encourage children to check that everyone in the group has got the same number. If not, ask them how can they make the numbers the same.

The story of Noah's Ark is a good introduction to the idea of counting in pairs.

Opportunities for working with pairs, sharing practically, halving single items and numbers of things

Incidental activity

Food

Sharing snacks, treats, fruit or the proceeds of cooking all provide opportunities for the discussion of 'more', 'less' and 'the same as', as well as reasons to use the language of fractions.

Clothes

Clothes often come in pairs: wellies; gloves; socks pegged on a line. All these can be counted in either ones or twos.

Preparations

Preparing for various activities can involve counting in groups. For example, making books requires everyone to have two pieces of card for the cover, and a certain number of sheets of paper each to make pages.

Gardening

Bulbs and seeds can be shared out between plant pots. How many are left over?

Counting pairs of hands.

Whole group activity

Stories

Stories about pairs, such as Noah's Ark, are useful for demonstrating the patterns associated with division, multiplication, counting in twos, halving and doubling. Support this learning by asking children to act out the stories using props, puppets, pictures, and plastic or wooden numerals.

Rhymes

Rhymes such as 'Five Little Speckled Frogs' can be made more challenging: change the number of frogs to ten, with two frogs jumping away at a time. Magnet board figures can be used to record the starting number, and the frogs can be re-grouped into those in the pool and those still on the log.

Children can use their fingers to help them hold the numbers in their minds.

Finding partners

Activities that involve finding partners can be used to discuss sharing and pairing: "There are six children — how many pairs will that be?"; "There are nine children — will anyone be left over?".

Counting hands

Count how many hands, eyes, feet, or ears there are altogether in the group. This gives practice in counting in twos. Count fingers or toes to give the children practice in counting in fives or tens.

Multiplication, division, fractions
Activity: The Doorbell Rang

Children will experience

◆ sharing into equal groups

◆ rearranging a number in different ways

◆ counting

◆ comparing

◆ counting groups

Equipment

◆ a copy of *The Doorbell Rang* by Pat Hutchins

◆ playdough biscuits

◆ plates

Getting started

Read the story, then help the children to enact it with plates and playdough biscuits, or a magnet board or felt board with appropriate pictures.

Try sharing the biscuits out very unfairly so that the children discuss this and are encouraged to re-distribute them equally.

Questions to ask the children

Suppose there are six biscuits and two children, then someone else comes so there are three children ...

How many will they get each?

Suppose there are eight biscuits and two children ...
How many will they get each?
What about if there were ten biscuits? Twelve biscuits?

Suppose you have two biscuits on each plate and there are six biscuits,
How many children can have a plate?
What about if there are ten biscuits?

Suppose you have nine biscuits and two children ...
How many will they get each?

What to look for . . .

Multiplication, division, fractions	the children may . . .	if so . . .	Patterns and problems generally
	not share them fairly	discuss the need for each person to have the same number	
		do some activities from the 'Comparing' section	comparing
	deal one at a time	do some activities from the 'Counting for a Purpose' section	
sharing by estimating	use estimating rather than counting	this shows good use of subitising if the estimations are accurate; try larger numbers which require counting	
		check that they are able to use this logic to deal with two at a time	
sharing by dealing	count to check	this is a good use of counting; see if they are able to deal with bigger numbers	
			counting for a purpose
pairs	count pairs as units and talk about 'two threes'	this is quite sophisticated; chech whether they are able to count pairs in other contexts, or other sizes of pairs	
		try taking another number such as 18 to split up into equal groups	
fractions	suggest sharing one left over by dividing in half	discuss other contexts for fractions	
adding one or two	suggest dealing with a remainder by adding or subtracting to 'make it fair'	this shows practical application of the 'one more than' relationship	

Checklist — *keeping track of learning*

Counting

The number sequence: *can children . . .*

- tell you some of the number names?
- recite numbers in order to 3, 5, 10, 20? Above 20?
- say what number comes next?
  (for example, say "five" when asked "What comes after four?")

Organising counting: *can children . . .*

- coordinate saying numbers with pointing at objects?

Purposes for counting: *can children . . .*

- use counting spontaneously to check or to compare?

Understanding counting: *can children . . .*

- say how many there are after counting?
- count out a given number of objects from a larger number?
  (for example, give you five pennies out of a handful)

Representing numbers

Recognising numerals: *can children . . .*

- say what number you are pointing to?

Linking numerals to amounts: *can children . . .*

- match a wooden or plastic numeral to a number of objects?
- press a number on the computer to match a display of a number of objects?
- show the right number of fingers when you show them a numeral?

Recording numbers for a purpose: *can children . . .*

- make the right number of marks or pictures to show a number?
  (for example, the score in a game)
- read the numerals on a label to find out the answer to "How many ..."?

Forming numerals: *can children . . .*

- write numbers correctly?

Checklist

Number patterns and problems

Patterns in number: *can children . . .*

- spot patterns in saying numbers?
  (for example, carry on after 'twenty-one, twenty-two ...'
  or count 'twenty-nine, twenty-ten'?
- spot repeating numerals on number lines and 100-squares?

Estimating: *can children . . .*

- recognise how many objects there are without counting
  (or 'subitising')?
- give an approximate number for a collection?

Comparing: *can children . . .*

- use the language 'more than', 'fewer than', 'some' and
  'the same as'?
- compare two sets by eye, looking and estimating rather
  than counting?
- compare two sets by pairing one to one, and saying when
  one set has 'spare' items that can't be paired?
- compare two sets by counting and say which one has more?

Addition and subtraction: *can children . . .*

- use and explain strategies such as putting together,
  or removing some?
- talk about how many there are altogether, and how many left?
- predict the result of adding one, two or three objects to a set?
- predict the result of subtracting one, two or three objects
  from a set?
- count on or back from a number?

Multiplication, division and fractions: *can children . . .*

- arrange a set of objects in pairs?
- count pairs, saying "two, four, six"? or "one, two, three pairs"?
- share a set of objects fairly between more than two people?
- spot unequal halves?

BEAM would like to thank the following people for their contribution to the development of *Number in the Nursery and Reception*:

Mel Ahmet and Thornhill Primary School, London
Sophia Akhtar and Pooles Park Infant School, London
Nick Blackburn and Charles Lamb Primary School, London
Catherine Clark and Prior Weston Primary School, London
Mary Coen, Ann Bridges, Carole Skinner and All Saints CE Primary School, Carshalton
John Coggin and Downhills Junior School, London
Joanne Conduit, St John's Primary School, London
Shelagh Cosgrow and St Ursula's Infant School, Romford
Julia Cummings and Binsted Primary School, Alton
Karen Jones and Barton Moss Primary School, Eccles
Alison McGee and Falconbrook Primary School, London
Adèle Markey and Bury & Whitefield Jewish Primary School, Lancashire
Zubeida Meer and Kingsgate Infant and Nursery School, Kilburn
Catie Palfremann and Selwyn Primary School, London
Neil Ringrose and Langtons Infant School, Hornchurch
Chris Smith and Orchard Way Primary School, Croydon
John Spooner and Rotherfield Junior School, London
Lis Stuart and Grange Infant School, Daventry
Kathy Swallow and St Luke's Primary School, London
Ann Todd and Beech Street CP School, Eccles
Susie Weeds and Tufnell Park Primary School, London
The staff and children of Kate Greenaway Nursery, London